A Day at the Pumpkin Patch

Text by Megan Faulkner

Photographs by Adam Krawesky

Scholastic Inc.

New York Toronto London Auckland Sydney
Mexico City New Delhi Hong Kong Buenos Aires

For Melissa, Jen and Gus.
— M.F.

Acknowledgments: A very special thanks to the staff at Andrews' Scenic Acres, including Elaine for all of her help coordinating our visit and our knowledgeable guide, Doreen. To Frank Whittamore and the staff at Whittamore's Farm, thank you for sharing your farm with our photographer. Thank you to the staff and students at St. Gabriel School for letting us join their tour and for being such great models. And lastly, we'd like to thank the Windsor-West Hants Pumpkin Festival for letting us use their impressive giant pumpkin photos, and Dr. George Bassel, Ph.D., for his pumpkin expertise!

ISBN-13: 978-0-439-90010-2
ISBN-10: 0-439-90010-7

Photo credits: p. 21 "Pumpkin Weigh-in" and "Pumpkin Regatta" both © Windsor-West Hants Pumpkin Festival and back cover, "Be the Pumpkin" © Jason Colak.
Text copyright © 2006 by Megan Faulkner. Photographs (excluding those mentioned above) copyright © 2006 by Adam Krawesky. All rights reserved. Published by Scholastic Inc. SCHOLASTIC and associated logos are trademarks and/or registered trademarks of Scholastic Inc.

12 11 10 9 8 7 6 5 4   8 9 10 11/0

Printed in the U.S.A.   08

This edition first printing, October 2006

Autumn is nearly over. Nature is getting ready for winter,
but there is still much to see at the farm!

2

We love the sweet, crisp apples,
colorful decorative corn, plump
autumn raspberries, and most of all…

3

PUMPKINS!

This is our guide. She will show us different kinds of pumpkins,
explain how they grow, and tell us about the ways people use them.

We climb aboard a wagon so the tractor can pull us out to the pumpkin patch.

Small pie pumpkins are the first to ripen and be harvested.

Though all pumpkins can be eaten, only some types actually taste good. Sweet pie pumpkins are the best choice for making delicious pumpkin treats.

Because they're small, pie pumpkins are also the easiest to carry.
We each get to pick one to take home.

These tiny fruits are gourds. They are pumpkins'
funny-looking cousins. Gourds and pumpkins are
both members of the squash family.

We have a contest to see who can find the strangest-looking gourd!

Next we visit the
patch that has the
pumpkins we know
best — the ones that
will become
jack-o'-lanterns.

Much bigger than pie pumpkins, these pumpkins are too heavy for us to lift by ourselves.

It's hard to believe they grew from tiny pumpkin seeds!

We gather round to learn more about pumpkins.

Fruit can grow in four different ways: on a tree, bush, cane, or vine. Pumpkins grow on vines. The large leaves stand on tall stalks and reach toward the sun. Once a pumpkin is ripe, the leaves turn brown and shrivel up.

14

A stem, or peduncle, connects a pumpkin to the vine. Water and nutrients from the earth and sun travel along the vine and enter the pumpkin through the stem. This gives the pumpkin the energy it needs to grow.

The thin curlicues attached to the stem are called tendrils. They wrap themselves around rocks and other objects to keep the plant safely in one place.

On the bottom of the pumpkin is a circle; it's called the blossom end. Before there was a pumpkin, there was a flower. When the flower was pollinated and the pumpkin began to grow, the flower dried up and fell off. The circle is what's left of the flower.

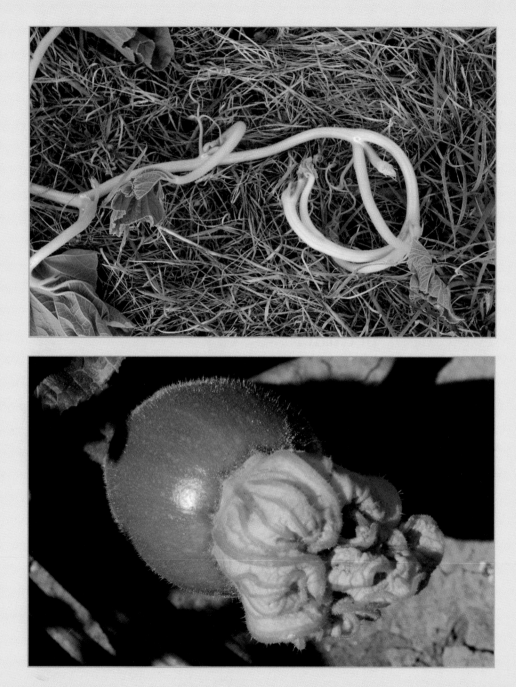

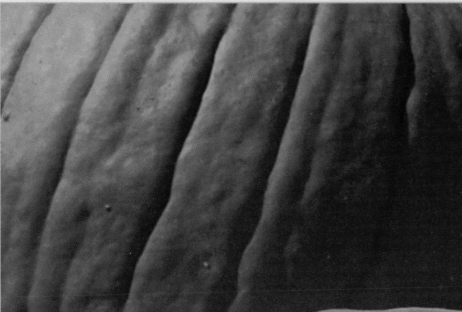

The pumpkin's shiny orange skin is called the rind. It protects the pumpkin from disease and insects. Inside the rind is an orange pulp — the tasty part used in baking and cooking.

The lines that run up and down on the pumpkin are called ribs. Depending on the pumpkin, there can be many ribs or just a few.

They are put on display so that visitors to the farm can choose the one they'd like to take home.

Since pumpkins are heavy, farmers load them onto wagons and pull them out of the patch with tractors. Now that they've been harvested, it's easier to protect them if the weather gets too cold.

There are so many! Which one will make the best jack-o'-lantern?

The biggest pumpkin of all is the Atlantic Giant. Not only is it the largest pumpkin, it is the biggest fruit on earth!

Often weighing in at more than eight hundred pounds, these giants are grown for competition at pumpkin festivals and country fairs. Since giant pumpkins are about 90 percent water, they aren't good for eating, but they make great jack-o'-lanterns — and boats!

We've learned a lot about pumpkins. Now we get to have some other fall fun.

There's a haunted forest and a play area made of hay!

Our tour of the farm is over. We can't
wait to get home and carve our pumpkins!

Once your pumpkin is clean and dry, the fun can begin!

Draw a face on the side of the pumpkin that has the fewest bumps and bruises. Ask an adult to cut a circle around the stem. This will be your lid.

Now it's time to pull out all the strands and seeds. They're cold and slimy. We save the seeds to make a special snack later.

When only the shell is left, carve out the face you drew. Now it's a real jack-o'-lantern!

Roasted Pumpkin Seeds

People have been snacking on pumpkin seeds for thousands of years.
They are nutritious and taste great roasted!

Ingredients:
- Seeds of one pumpkin
- Olive oil
- ½ teaspoon of salt

1) Pre-heat oven to 350° Fahrenheit.

2) Wash the seeds thoroughly in warm water — make sure all the pumpkin gunk is gone.

3) Spread the seeds out on a paper towel and let them dry completely.

4) In a bowl, toss the seeds with olive oil.

26

7) Ask an adult to put them in the oven for 20 minutes, stirring every five minutes. The seeds are done when they are dry and golden.

Cool and serve.

5) Spread the seeds on a cookie sheet.

6) Sprinkle them with salt or other flavoring.

Variations:
Be creative with your pumpkin seeds! Here are a few seasoning suggestions:

Cayenne pepper	Garlic salt
Sugar and cinnamon	Cheese popcorn seasoning
Powdered taco seasoning	Soy sauce
Cajun seasoning mix	Curry powder

Pumpkin Facts

- Pumpkins are members of the Cucurbit family, which includes gourds, squash, melons, cucumbers, zucchini, and even loofah. (Yes, that spongy thing you use in the bathtub!)

- In North America most jack-o'-lanterns are made from Connecticut Field and Howden's Field pumpkins.

- Pumpkins aren't just orange. They can be pale green, white, terra-cotta, pale yellow, dark green, and even blue!

- Pumpkin flowers are edible.

- Never let your pumpkin get a chill. Temperatures less than 32° F will cause a pumpkin to rot.

- Pumpkins are orange because they are rich in beta-carotene (just like carrots), which turns into vitamin A in your body.

- One of the wonderful things about pumpkins is that you can grow them right in your own backyard in one season. Pumpkin seeds planted in the garden in late May or early June can produce a jack-o'-lantern–sized pumpkin by October.

- In the past, people believed pumpkins could get rid of freckles!

- Pumpkin chunking is a sport. Teams build machines designed to throw a pumpkin as far as possible.

Historical Note

Pumpkins have been grown in North America for thousands of years. Native Peoples ate it dried, fresh, or cooked. It was boiled, baked in hot ashes, or added to other dishes. They also wove strips of dried pumpkin to make mats.

In 1535, while traveling with the Iroquois of Hochelaga (now Montreal), Jacques Cartier saw what he described as "pepon." Back at home, the French changed it to "pompon" and the English adapted that to "pumpion." Colonists in the new world changed it one last time to "pumpkin." They learned to grow pumpkins from Native Peoples, and adapted the cooking techniques to suit their own diet.

The tradition of carving pumpkins comes from an Irish legend. At the end of the old Celtic year, October 31, households would put a candle in a hollowed-out turnip or similar vegetable, and place it outside their door to scare off evil spirits. One well-known spirit, Stingy Jack, is the origin of the name jack-o'-lantern. Irish immigrants brought the custom to North America, where they discovered that a pumpkin was the perfect form for a jack-o'-lantern.

Notes

Pollination of Pumpkin Flowers:

🎃 Pumpkins have many male flowers and some female flowers. Only female flowers can be pollinated to make pumpkins.

🎃 The flowers are pollinated by insects, especially beetles. The pumpkin plant starts making male flowers long before it makes the female ones. This attracts hungry insects who want to feed on the pollen and nectar. Once there are lots of insects around the vine, female flowers begin to grow.

🎃 Now the insects can spread the pollen between the male and female flowers. They crawl from one flower to the next, feeding on nectar and carrying pollen along with them from male to female flowers.

🎃 Pumpkin flowers close at night and open in the morning. Sometimes hungry insects can get trapped inside a flower for the night!